ANDREW MARTIN

Interior Design Review Volume 15

teNeues

You can stage a lively debate about which part of the world has impacted design most. Ancient Greece has a powerful claim with the echoes of its noble classicism still all around us. Renaissance Italy has defined our attitude to art and so much more for the past 500 years. One cannot exclude the advocates for the France of Louis XIV, when decoration reached its zenith at Versailles. Cases can be made for the Arab world of the Middle Ages, Georgian England or even Bauhaus Germany.

However, there is a strong argument that China has been more influential than anywhere else. From the development of silk to the invention of its eponymous porcelain, for 2000 years cargoes of Chinese goods have been decorating the homes of the world. But more than this, the Chinese style of design has been a powerful force. As soon as Marco Polo saw the luxury of the Grand Khan's stately pleasure domes in 1265, western attitudes were destined to change. The Chinese sway reached its peak in 18th century Europe. In England, Chinese Chippendale and the Prince Regent's Brighton Pavilion are the most obvious examples. In France, Chinoiserie was an essential component of the great châteaux of the time. Louis XIV was a particular fan. At Chantilly, whole rooms were elaborate homages to Chinoiserie.

Much more recently the vogue for all things Chinese returned. The 1990s saw a proliferation of lacquer trunks, wedding cabinets and blue and white vases. East meets West was the buzz mantra. However this was really just a retrospective of greatest hits from the Tang and Ming eras of centuries before. In general, beyond Andy Warhol's Mao, the 20th century was not an age of new inspiration from China.

However, today the economic boom in China is proving to be fertile soil for a remarkable comeback for Chinese design. A new wave of designers are exploding onto the scene and their approach is set to define a new look for the 21st century.

Martin Waller

Rabih Hage

Company: Rabih Hage, London. Rabih Hage is an architect, designer, curator. He has established himself as a reference in new hotel concepts and developments, working with international hoteliers, developers and private clients. Recent projects include the concept for a Berlin hotel/residence for artists and collectors, the concept for a beach hotel in Catalunya mixing historical elements of the existing building with a modern extension and an apartment in Paris with an international blend of objects and art. Current work includes a Radisson Edwardian Hotel, front of house interiors including the lobby, lounge, bar, bistro and restaurant. Rabih has also developed the concept for a new approach to the mass market luxury hotel making it more personal and the interior spaces more accessible. He is working on various residential projects in the UK and internationally.

Beijing Newsdays

Designers: Jianguo Liang, Wenqi Cai, Yiqun Wu, Junye Song, Zhenhua Luo, Chunkai Nie, Eryong Wang. Company: Beijing Newsdays Architectural Design Co. China. Established 25 years ago and recognised for its design of the international reception space at the Beijing Olympic Games. Along with China's largest real estate company Newsdays has also served international brand stores like Versace, Armani, and Walter Knoll. Recent work includes the five star Lakeview Hotel (part of Peking University, Beijing), Trend Tower, Beijing and Yiquande Private Club House, Beijing. Current work includes the Club House Of The Forbidden City, Beijing.

Kelly Hoppen

Company: Kelly Hoppen, London. Kelly began her business at the age of 16 and in 2009 received an MBE for her services to Interior Design. As well as designing apartments, houses and yachts for an ever-expanding international private client list, Kelly also undertakes commercial design projects including hotels, restaurants, office spaces and notably the interiors for British Airways' first class cabins. She shares her knowledge in the Kelly Hoppen Design School, designs a range of home accessories and has a highly successful QVC range. Her seven books have been translated into numerous foreign languages and her work has graced the covers of magazines worldwide. The art of display is fundamental to Kelly's design philosophy.

Salomé Gunter

Company: Salomé Gunter Interiors, Cape Town, South Africa. Bespoke, domestic and corporate projects. Recent work includes a family residence in Johannesburg, new premises for Pernod Ricard in Cape Town and a holiday cottage in Churchaven, one of South Africa's most unique bird sanctuaries. Current projects include the renovation of a historic building into a contemporary home in Tamboerskloof, Cape Town, the restoration of a barn in the heart of Franschhoek and the renovation of a 12th century bastide in the Dordogne, France.

Company: Ola Laska, Warsaw, Poland. A small practice specialising in interior design and architecture predominantly in Poland. Recent work is in Warsaw and includes a loft conversion for an actor in the old town, a pied a terre and a house. Current projects include a studio and a large showroom.

Aleksandra Laska

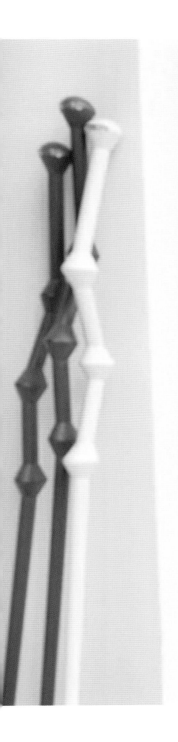

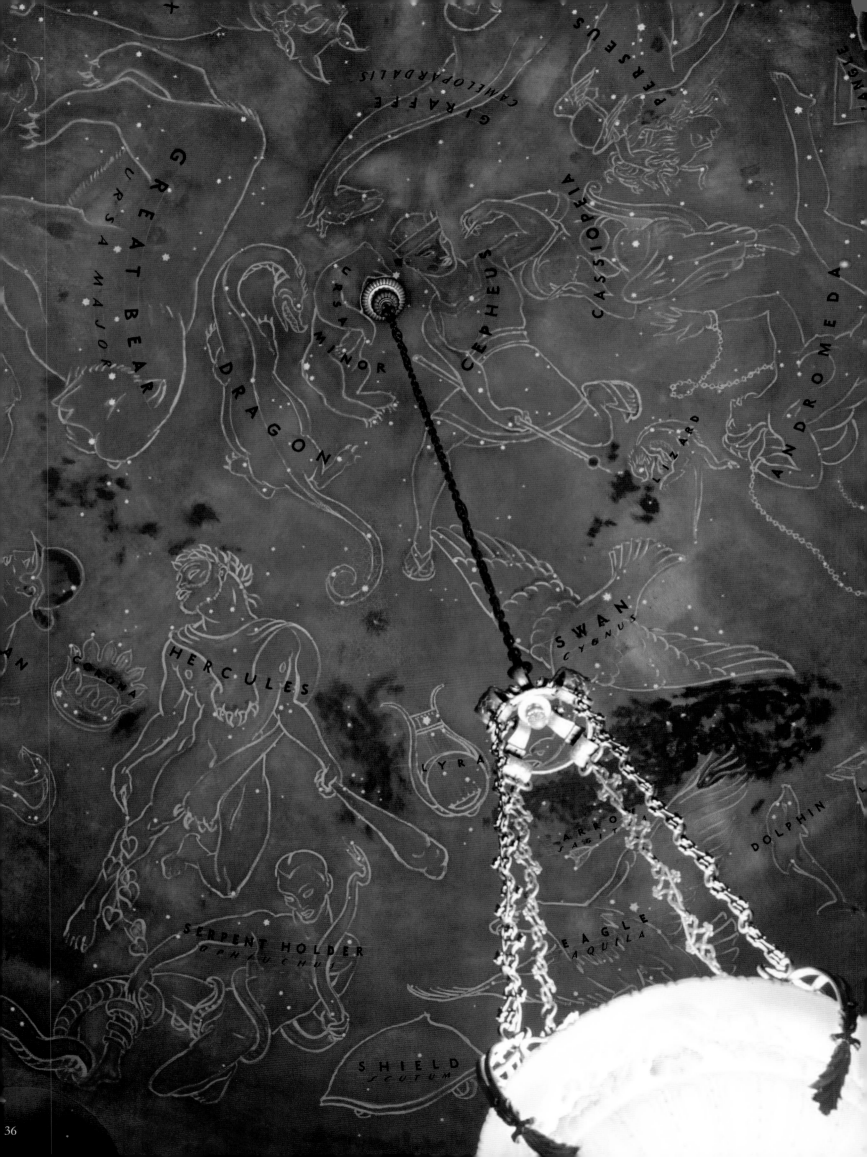

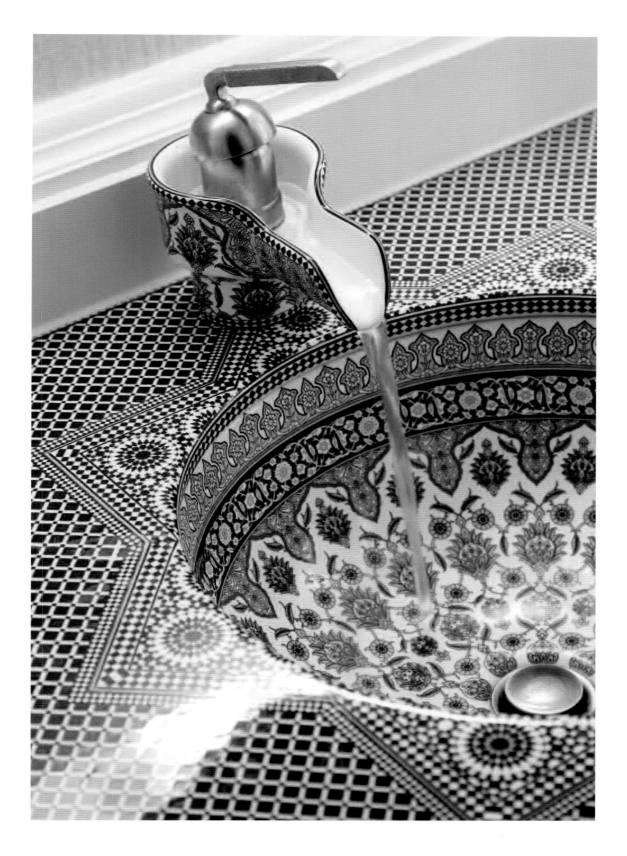

Alexandra Champalimaud

Company: Champalimaud, Montreal, Canada. The company has established itself as a leader in hospitality design with the renovations of The Drake Hotel, The Carlyle and the Gold Key award winning renovation of the iconic Algonquin Hotel. Today Champalimaud have been privileged to work on many of New York's most successful hotels. Recent projects include The Green Leaf Niseko Village, Hokkaido, Japan, The Astor Hotel, Tianjin, China and The Fairmont San Francisco Penthouse, CA. Current work includes Hotel Bel Air, Los Angeles, The Dorchester, London and The Carlyle, New York.

Pamela Makin

Company: Les Interieurs, Sydney, Australia. A small design practice known for creating unique interiors. Recent projects include a waterfront estate in Sydney's Palm Beach, a three level resort house on Scotland Island and the complete restoration of a beach house overlooking the Pacific Ocean. Current work includes a contemporary 4 bedroom residence overlooking Lion Island, a pied a terre in the heart of Sydney and the entire refurbishment of an estate in Vaucluse and another in Balmoral.

Ichiro Nishiwaki

Company: Ichiro Nishiwaki Design Office, Tokyo, Japan. Established in 1991, specialising in interior design, architecture, furniture design, branding, MD consulting and graphic design planning. Recent work includes a shop and gallery selling Japanese dolls, a coffee shop and a vintage clothing store.

Nicky Dobree

Company: Nicky Dobree Interior Design, London. A small practice specialising in luxury ski chalets and high end private residential projects. Recent work includes a London townhouse, a chalet in Switzerland and a family country house. Current projects include a chalet in St Moritz, a villa in Italy and a London townhouse. Nicky's design philosophy is about retaining the soul of a building and creating a home that is comfortable and harmonious.

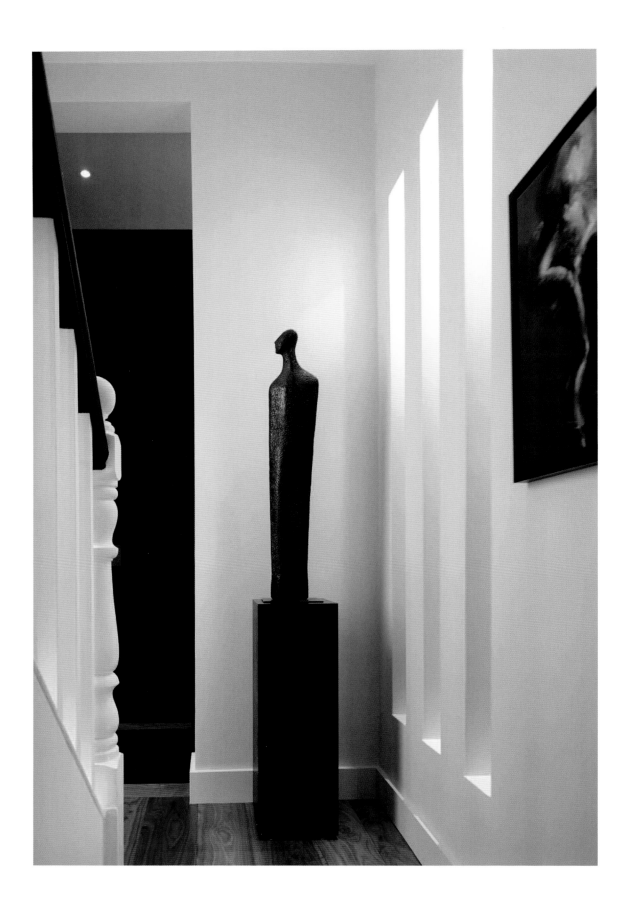

Nicola Fontanella

Company: Argent Design, London. Argent Design provides an international service for private residences, aircraft and super yachts. Current work includes a luxury property development in Barbados, prestigious apartments in Monaco and New York and several high end developments in London's most exclusive areas.

Claire Cicaloni

Designers: Claire Cicaloni & Philippe Sarda. Company: Claire Cicaloni Interior Design, Vesenaz, Switzerland. Specialising in the development, creation and decoration of private, public, interior and exterior spaces. 2011 saw the opening of a new office in Buenos Aires. Recent work includes restaurant Le Petit Lac in Corsier and a swimming pool and offices in Geneva. Current projects include a flat in La Capite, Geneva, a house in the country and a flat in Buenos Aires. Claire's Italian roots give her projects a unique feel, mixing styles using simple and sober materials, decorated with warm colours and fabrics.

Lynne Hunt

Company: Lynne Hunt London. A small practice specialising in the hotel and leisure industry as well as residential design. Recent work encompasses Laucala Island, Fiji, Mont Chalet, Verbier and the London Hilton Park Lane. Current projects include Karma Lakelands Golf Club House, New Delhi, Hyatt Regency The Churchill, London and Jumeirah Carlton Tower, London. Lynne's design philosophy is to develop interiors based on brief, location and client expectation. Having travelled extensively, it is her collection of artefacts and accessories along with a great attention to detail that bring a new sense of place to her projects.

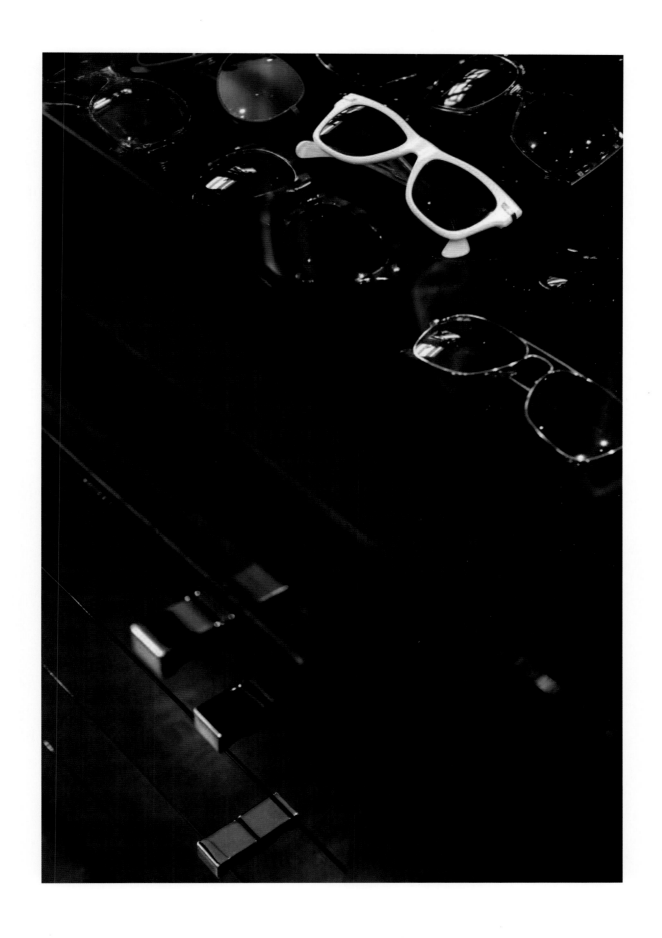

Katharine Pooley

Company: Katharine Pooley Limited, London. Specialising in high end commissions for landmark commercial and residential projects worldwide. Recent work includes the redesign of a 19th century mews house in Hyde Park, the transformation of a penthouse for an international private client in Park Lane, Mayfair and the classical redesign of an 18th century country estate in Gloucestershire. Current projects include a large contemporary apartment in the heart of Singapore, a palace with extensive private gardens and spa in Kuwait and the Royal suites at Heathrow airport.

Christian Baumann

Company: Abraxas Interiors, Zürich, Switzerland. Abraxas focus on distinctive, custom made interiors. Recent projects include a 20 room villa with pool and spa area at the Gold Coast in Zürich, a store design for an international fashion chain and the design for a lounge restaurant in the Swiss mountains. Current work includes a 124 ft yacht in Italy and a mountain apartment in Switzerland. Christian's philosophy on design is to make the ordinary extraordinary by evoking an emotional response. He thinks that designers are meant to be loved, not understood and that good design can be planned but great design just happens.

Ryu Kosaka

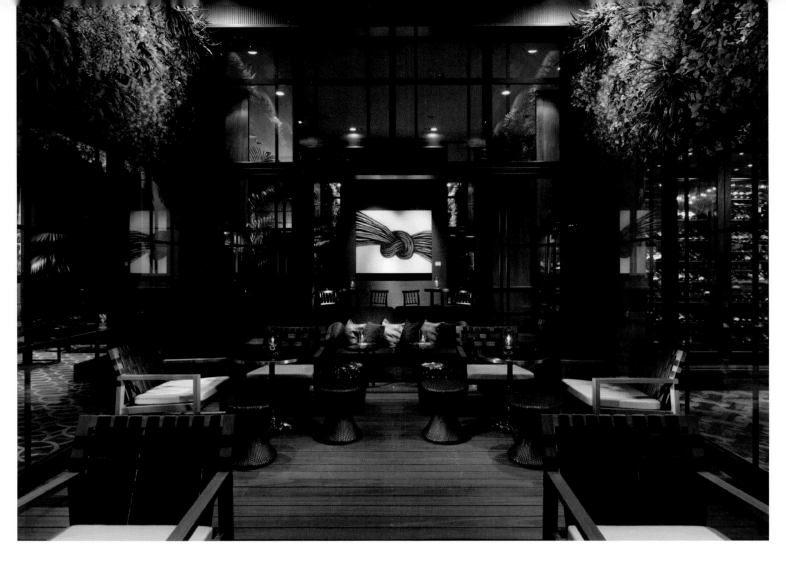

Company: A.N.D., Tokyo, Japan. Specialising in high end commercial, residential and product design predominantly in Japan. Recent work includes the Mandarin Oriental sushi restaurant 'Sora' in Tokyo, Namba Dining Maison in Namba, Osaka and David Myers Café in Ginza, Tokyo. Current projects include the bar design at W Hotel Gangzhou, the lounge and bar design at Hotel Galaxy, Macau and the refurbishment of the restaurant at Sheshan International Golf Club. Their motto is 'everlasting design.'

Hecker Guthrie

Designers: Paul Hecker & Hamish Guthrie. Company: Hecker Guthrie, Melbourne, Australia. A multi disciplinary practice under the direction of Paul Hecker and Hamish Guthrie. Projects are local and international within the hospitality, residential, retail and commercial sectors. Recent work includes The Millswyn Restaurant located opposite Melbourne's famed Botanical gardens, Graze & Kha (two adjoining hospitality projects) situated in a former warehouse in the old 'godown'

district of Singapore and a Caulfield residence, a 60's family home in Melbourne. Current projects include Frangipani restaurant located in a Sir Norman Foster building in KL, Grace restaurant in Adelaide and a series of private residential projects in Melbourne and Sydney. Driven by the principles of authenticity, consideration and enthusiasm, Hecker Guthrie's approach is to create a unique identity for each project using a natural palette of materials.

Blainey North

Company: Blainey North Associates, Sydney, Australia. An architecture and design company specialising in bespoke projects. Recent work includes the presidential suite at the Intercontinental in Perth, the presidential suite and villas at

Crown Towers Hotel in Melbourne, and Riley St Film Studios in Sydney. Current projects include Kings Park Road Gallery in Perth, the renovation of the Intercontinental Hotel in Perth and The Crystal Club Lounge in Melbourne. Blainey North have also recently designed a new furniture and lighting collection.

Pippa Paton

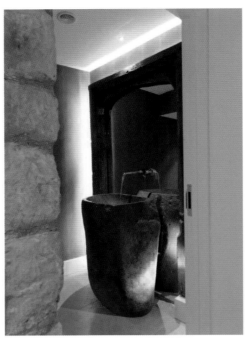

Company: Pippa Paton Design, UK. Known for unusual pieces and eclectic designs, Pippa Paton Design offer a bespoke renovation and project management service. Recent work includes a 16th century manor house in Oxfordshire, a swimming pool and leisure complex and an historic Thames river boat. Current work includes a 17th century estate. 'Instinct is everything, rules are nothing.'

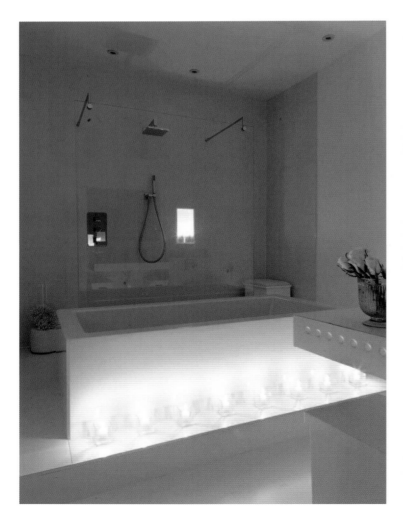

Oficinas da Casa

Designers: Anabela Hipolito and Vitor Maciel. Company: Oficinas da Casa, Esposende, Portugal. A family business founded by Anabela Hipolito and Vitor Maciel. Working with a team of professionals, they specialise in private residences. Recent projects include the sensitive restoration of their new premises, an early 20th century house. Current work includes an ongoing project for a fashion boutique and two large residential projects beside the sea.

Irina Dymova

Company: Irina Dymova Design Studio, Moscow, Russia. Specialising in country residences and city apartments as well as public spaces predominantly in Russia. Recent work includes a high end beauty salon, a country house and apartments in Moscow.

Anemone Wille Vage

Company: AWV Interiør AS, Oslo, Norway. A small company specialising in the interiors of private residences and chalets as well as restaurants and hotels in Norway and internationally. Recent work includes Theatercaféen in Oslo, which opened in 1900 and is today listed as one of the ten most famous cafés in the world, the complete renovation of a private villa in Oslo and a large office space for Pangea Property Partners in Stockholm. Current projects include the transformation of a 1920's post hall in Gothenburg into a luxury, modern 500 room hotel including breakfast hall, bar, lounges and restaurant due to reopen in 2012. Recent work includes the refurbishment of the Hotel Tjuvholmen, situated beside the sea in central Oslo and the expansion of the historical Hotel Union Øye in Alesund, Norway.

Simon Mcilwraith

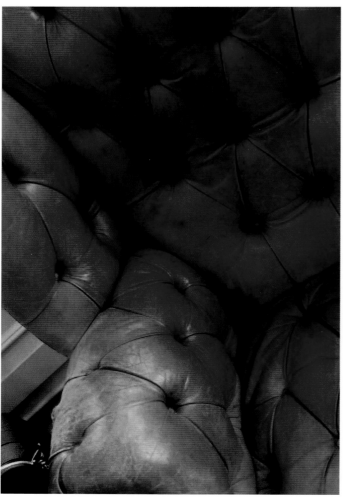

Company: Collective Design, Newcastle, UK. Luxury commercial design, including bars, restaurants, hotels and retail environments. Current projects include a bar and restaurant in Lucerne, a boutique designer clothing store in Glasgow and a hair and beauty salon in Newcastle. Recent work includes nightclubs in Sheffield and Leeds, a number of high end multi branded designer fashion projects throughout the UK and a hotel wine bar.

Gorozhankin Architects Studio

Designers: Andrey Gorozhankin, Maria Gorozhankina & Uriy Ryntovt. Company: Gorozhankin Architects Studio, Moscow. Specialising in private and commercial interiors predominantly in Moscow. Recent work includes a boutique, Monika Ricchi in Moscow, a restaurant, 'Cafe April' in Moscow and a hotel build in Murmansk. Current projects include a country residence housing complex, the reconstruction and interior of a private house and an apartment, all in Moscow.

Lucia Valzelli

Company: Dimore di Lucia Valzelli, Brescia, Italy. An individual design practice specialising in high end bespoke projects including hotels and spas. Recent work includes a fully equipped botanical garden complete with tool shed, part of a private villa and important corporate headquarters in an historical

mansion, the renovation of an 800 sq m private residence in the heart of the city and a series of interior design and furnishing projects for residential villas. Current projects include the complete renovation of a 1930's villa and spa on Lake Garda, the full refurbishment and interior of a mountain home and the design and build of a glasshouse on a city centre penthouse roof garden.

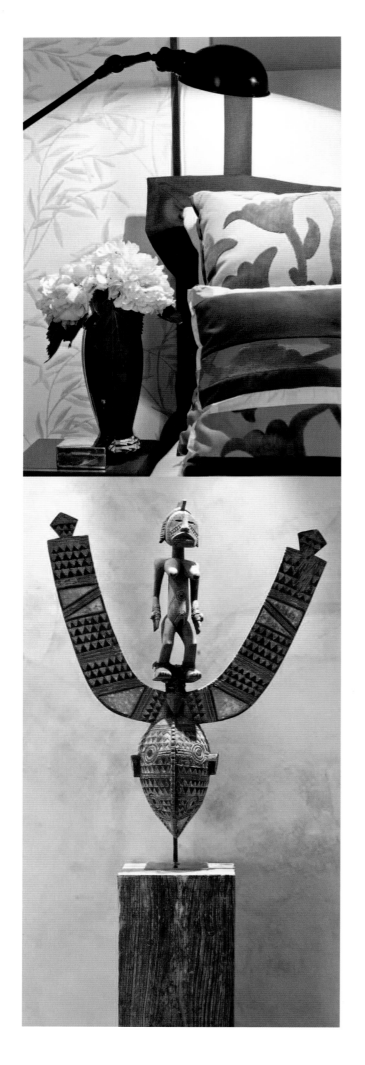

George Efthimiou

Company: George Efthimiou, Athens, Greece. Established in Athens twenty years ago, George Efthimiou specialises in interior decoration for private houses, offices and yachts in Europe and the Middle East. Recent work includes The Elounda Beach Hotel and a private yacht 'Falcon'. Current projects include Elysium Hotel, Mykonos, an apartment in London and an office building in Athens.

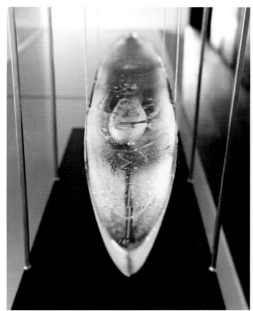

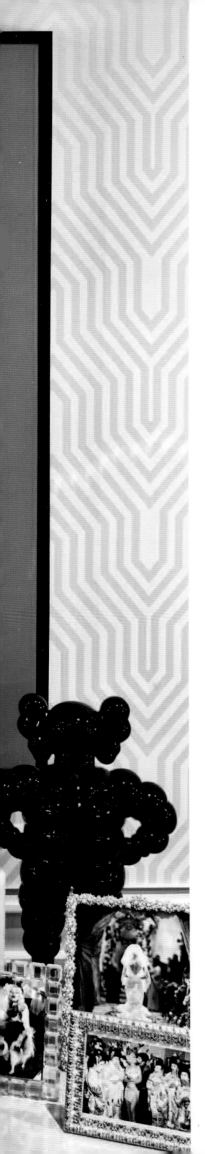

Woodson & Rummerfield's

Designers: Ron Woodson & Jamie Rummerfield, Los Angeles, U.S.A. Specialising in interiors for a dynamic clientele worldwide, they have also introduced W&R Home to their brand; a whimsical and fashion-led collection of furniture, wallpaper and accessories. Recent projects include Christina Aguilera's Beverly Hills Estate, Courtney Love's Los Angeles homes and the restoration of Richard Neutra's Bonnet house in Hollywood. Current work includes multiple projects in the Ritz-Carlton Residences Tower in Los Angeles, Courtney Love's West Village townhouse, NY, Greystone Maison de Luxe Showcase house and 'Mrs. Doheny's bedroom' Greystone Historic Mansion, Beverly Hills. Woodson & Rummerfield's design philosophy is based on a deep rooted appreciation for Hollywood history, the California landscape and the 'high style' inherent in a city steeped in groundbreaking culture, architecture and design.

Designers: Irina Mavrodieva & Arthur Goga. Company: A.M.G. Project, Moscow. Specialising in private apartments, houses, public spaces, restaurants, spas, offices and hotels. Recent work includes a conceptual white apartment. A.M.G's design philosophy is to unite architecture and art to create their client's dream.

A.M.G. Project

Susana Camelo

Company: Susana Camelo Interior Design, Porto, Portugal. Involved in all aspects of design for residential projects, show flats and boutique hotels. Current work includes private homes, one designed by award winning architect Eduardo Souto de Moura, plus a French gourmet tea house and a hotel concept. Recent projects include private and commercial work, a night club, Boavista Palace serviced apartments and a 1000 square metre beach house.

Stefano Dorata

Company: Stefano Dorata Architetto, Rome, Italy. A small practice specialising in private work internationally. Recent projects include a penthouse in Cortina, an apartment in New York and a villa in Portofino. Current work includes a villa in Israel, an apartment in Piazza di Spagna, Rome and two villas in Punta Ala. 'Have clear design rules in order to break them.'

Peter Phan

Company: Peter Phan Design Consultancy, London. Recent projects include a house and an apartment in Regent's Park and a country house in Oxfordshire. Current work includes a chateau and a golf course club house in France and a house in St John's Wood. 'Stylish and relevant but most of all comfortable.'

Constance Tew

Company: Creative Mind Design, Singapore. Led by creative director and founder Constance Tew, CMD specialise in show suites, predominantly in land scarce high rise private residences in Singapore. Experts of space planning, CMD Design have conceptualised and built more than one hundred luxurious show apartments within the last three years. Recent projects include Floridian, a high end residential condominium plus residential offices in Greenwich and The Tennery. Current work includes further high end residential condominiums including Scotts Tower, Eu-Habitat and Woodhaven.

Lesley Carstens

Company: Silvio Rech & Lesley Carstens Architecture & Interior Architecture, Johannesburg, South Africa. A small, award-winning architectural practice, specialising in lodges in Tanzania, Botswana and the Seychelles which have become forerunners in a new island and bush aesthetic.

Jumpei Yamagiwa

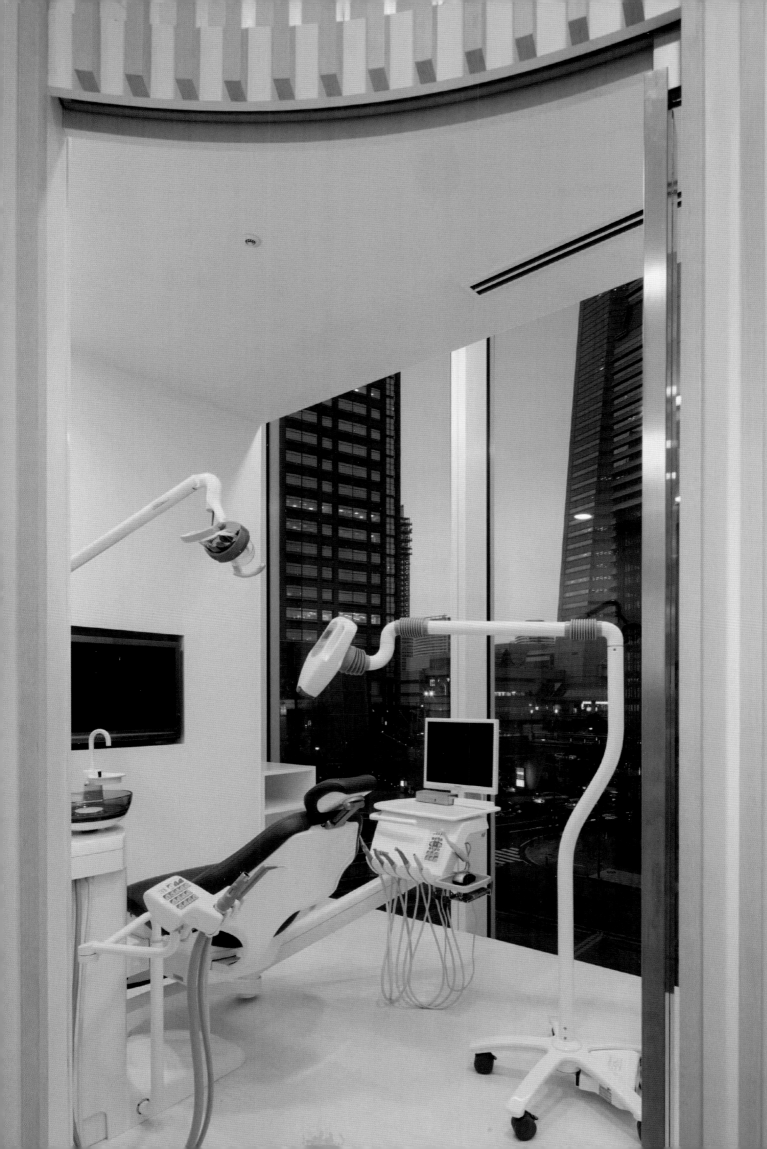

Company: Design Post, Tokyo, Japan. Specialising in the design of over 100 restaurants as fine dining and club lounges throughout Asia. Recent projects include Palace Hotel in Tokyo, a private club house in Hong Kong and Sky Club House residence in Hong Kong. Yamagiwa describes the company's design philosophy as flexible, whilst retaining the spirit of Japanese art and timeless design.

Atelier de L'Opera

Designers: Jean Turcotte & Louis Pepin. Company: Atelier de L'Opera, Quebec, Canada. Established over 25 years ago, Louis Pepin and Jean Turcotte specialise in prestigious large scale residential and commercial projects internationally. Elegance, comfort, precision and attention to detail are their hallmarks. Recent work includes a country house in Laurentides, a private residence in Ottawa and a downtown apartment in Montreal.

Jayne Wunder

Company: Jayne Wunder Interior Design, Dubai & Cape Town, South Africa. Current projects include a prestigious development and retreat on a private island off Abu Dhabi.

Robert Mills

Company: Robert Mills Architects and Interior Designers, Prahran, Australia. Specialising in award winning finely crafted sustainable buildings and interiors intended to serve generations. Recent work includes beach houses in Lorne and Sorrento plus a private house in Verdant Avenue, Melbourne. Current projects include private houses around Melbourne's premier inner city and coastal areas. Robert Mills Architects believe that good contemporary residential design in Australia should be 'sophisticated yet relaxed, featuring natural textured materials with furniture, rugs, artwork and objects that complement the architecture whilst expressing the owner's personality.'

Fabio Galeazzo

Company: Galeazzo Design, São Paulo, Brazil. Galeazzo Design specialise in creative, eco friendly projects for private and commercial clients. Recent work includes an apartment for a magazine editor, a pied a terre in São Paulo and a duplex penthouse in front of Ibirapuera Park. Current projects include a conceptual urban cottage for the release of a British car in Brazil, an eco village of guest houses for private clients and a contemporary house inspired by Venetian architecture. Philosophy: to make things beautiful.

Ligia Casanova

Company: Atelier Ligia Casanova, Lisbon, Portugal. Specialising in private and commercial interiors including corporate, business, fashion and hospital design plus scenography and art direction for films. Recent projects include houses in Oporto and Lisbon. Current work includes a beach house near Comporta, a hotel and a project in Shanghai.

Ivan Cheng

Company: Ivan C. Design Limited, Kwai Chung, Hong Kong. Founded in Hong Kong in 2001 by Cheng Si-Leung. Clients are predominantly hotels, villas, show flats and clubhouses. Recent work includes SkyCity Marriott Hotel, HK international airport, Yuyan Renaissance Hotel, Shanghai, XiXi Wangzhuang, China and a Shanghai apartment. Current projects are located in Hangzhou and include Hilton Hotel Qiandao

Lake, Bin Sheng Xiang-Lake Villas and Tien Wu villa and clubhouse. Unafraid of colour or unusual proportions, Ivan reinvents interiors into striking space by combining classic influences with Chinese style.

Sera of London

Designer: Sera Hersham Loftus. Company: Sera of London. Sera delivers unmistakably feminine interiors punctuated with eccentric antiques and artefacts. With her romantic use of lace and oversized black and white seductive photography, her work evokes the atmosphere of a 1970's David Hamilton film set in the South of France. Current projects include writing a book, The Seductive Interior, the decoration of the dressing room for 'the most famous showgirl this century' and the recording studio for a rock 'n' roll hero. Her design philosophy is 'to create a magic interior that draws together memories, cultures, psychology and vision.'

Petra Richards

Company: Petra Richards Interiors, Colorado, U.S.A. and Frankfurt, Germany. A boutique design practice specialising in private residential projects throughout the U.S.A. and Europe. Current work includes a residence in Denver, a restaurant and bar in Frankfurt and a ski chalet in Aspen. Recent projects include a beach house on the Costa Brava, Spain, a private residence at The Vintage Club in Palm Desert and a house in Bel Air.

T. K. Chu

Company: T. K. Chu Design Group, Taiwan. Exclusive residential and commercial design throughout major cities in China and Taiwan. Recent projects include Beijing global trade mansion Lee apt, Shanghai Star River A Unit and Xinhai Bay: The One Club. T. K. Chu's design philosophy is devotion to achieve excellence.

S. B. Interiors

Designers: Sandra Billington & Guillermo Estenoz. Company: S. B. Interiors, Malaga, Spain. Specialising in tailor made residential projects. Recent work includes a boutique hotel in Switzerland, a beach front house in Barbados, an apartment in Lugano and a property in Marbella.

Current projects include a house in Miami, a farm and chalet in Switzerland and various homes in southern Spain. Sandra's design philosophy is to create an eclectic atmosphere which excites the client, combining beauty, luxury and comfort.

Maria Kartashova

Company: Maria Kartashova Interior Design, Moscow. Work is predominantly high end residential with some commercial projects. Recent work includes a 600 sq m waterfront residence in Mallorca, a private apartment in the historical centre of Moscow and a restaurant in Moscow. Current projects include a 700 sq m restaurant complex in a hotel in Vladimir city and a 350 sq m private house. Maria's design philosophy is to make her client happy.

Candy & Candy

Designers: Nick & Christian Candy. Company: Candy & Candy, London. An internationally recognised company specialising in luxury, bespoke design in some of the world's most exclusive locations. Projects include the design of yachts, jets, luxury cars and a wide range of commercial environments as well as large and boutique residential properties in London. Commissions for private clients are as far reaching as Monaco, Spain, Italy, America, Russia, Qatar, Nigeria and Dubai. Recent work includes One Hyde Park: The Residences at Mandarin Oriental, London. Their vision for One Hyde Park was to create the most exquisite interiors for the most exclusive address in the world.

Prasetio Budhi

Company: Plus Design, Jakarta, Indonesia. Founded in 2003, Plus Design has grown substantially and attracted many high profile clients across the residential, retail and commercial sector. Recent work includes a house in Beverly Hills, a colonial inspired residence in central Java and the renovation of a ballroom in Jakarta. Current projects include traditional and French style homes and the executive office for an energy company all in Jakarta.

Eric Kuster

Company: Eric Kuster Metropolitan Luxury, The Netherlands. Preceded by a short time in fashion, Eric Kuster's design career began in textiles in 1989, when he took on the position of creative and commercial director of Dutch textile manufacturer Chivasso. Before long he was recognised by other style connoisseurs and offered the opportunity to open a shop in the upbeat town of Laren, NL. Specialising in high end furniture, lighting and textiles, the outlet quickly became a destination lifestyle store and inspired him to start his own label, 'Eric Kuster Metropolitan Luxury'. His signature style adorns many commercial enterprises and landmark locations such as the exclusive club Jimmy Woo in Amsterdam and the Barcelona Football Club stadium, the 'Nou Camp'. More recently Kuster has opened showrooms in Amsterdam, Dubai and Moscow, with Egypt and Slovenia soon to follow. His first mono brand store, offering turnkey services as well as his furniture and textiles range, opened in late 2009 in Ibiza and in 2010 the second store opened in Antwerp, Belgium.

Chang Ching-Ping

Company: Tien Fun Interior Planning, Taiwan. Established in 1988 Tien Fun specialise in award winning, high end residential and show flat design throughout Asia. Their team consists of more than 20 experienced designers working on varying styles of projects; from Asian to classic, modern to retro. Recent work includes a show flat for Wang Jin Yuan, Chengdu, China, the residential design for King's Vision apartment, Taichung, Taiwan and Tian Han apartment, Taichung, Taiwan.

Current projects include the club house for 'Mansion De Crillon' and 'The Glory' plus residential design for Grange Infinite. Tien Fun's design philosophy is to exceed their client's expectations.

Manuel Francisco Jorge

Company: Manuel Francisco Jorge Interior Design Studio, Lisbon, Portugal. Working together with a team of specialists, predominantly in Portugal, Manuel Francisco Jorge specialises in a personalised service covering various sectors such as offices, clinics, shops, private residences and public spaces. Recent work includes an apartment and a loft in Lisbon and a beach house in Cascais. Current projects include the head office for Auto Sueco/Volvo in Lisbon, an apartment in Madrid and a cottage in Alentejo.

Carl Emil Erikson

Company: Carl Emil Erikson Design, Stockholm, Sweden. Specialising in building visual identities for offices, hotels, restaurants and public meeting places. In home environments they create interiors which reflect the values of those who live there. Recent projects include three offices for Grayling Sweden AB (leading global public relation consultancy firm) in Gothenburg, Malmö and Stockholm, an office for Medge Production House Ltd (media company) in Notting Hill, London and a shop design for Älva London (clothing boutique) in Chelsea.

Milsom Hotels

Designer: Geraldine Milsom. Company: Milsom Hotels and Restaurants, Essex. Geraldine Milsom, director and in house designer of Milsom Hotels, is responsible for the unique identity and collective contemporary design feel throughout this group. Founded in 1952, the company comprises 4 hotels and 5 restaurants.

Cao Cheng

Company: Shenzhen Hope-Box Surroundings Design Corporation, Shenzhen, China. Founded in 2004, they have a team of 65 designers specialising in restaurants, clubhouses, hotels, museums and shopping malls, as well as exclusive residential complexes. Recent work includes Printemps department store, Xian, Alin Abalone Restaurant, Yanan and a high end residential development, Tianmukuojing.

S. B. Long Interiors

Designer: Susan Bednar Long. Company: S. B. Long Interiors, Connecticut, USA. An internationally recognised firm well-known for delivering tailored, crisp and sophisticated interiors. Its signature style is 'modern traditional' offering comfort and elegance. Recent work includes the redesign of a NYC townhouse for a prominent actor, a mountain home in Deer Valley, Utah and a townhouse in London. Recent projects include Owner's Suites onboard Oceania Cruise Lines flagships, an estate home in Greenwich, Connecticut and a country estate in Washington, Connecticut. 'Relaxed and graceful.'

Finchatton

Designers: Andrew Dunn & Alex Michelin. Company: Finchatton, London. Specialising in creating unique residences in some of the most exclusive addresses worldwide. Recent projects include the private commission of a 6500 sq ft apartment in Chelsea, the concept for which was old Hollywood glamour, the complete refurbishment of a 3700 sq ft private apartment overlooking Lake Lugano, Switzerland and a penthouse apartment in Mayfair which was restored to its original grandeur of previous eras. Current work includes a villa in St Tropez and houses in Los Angeles and London.

Michelle Pabarcius

Company: Design Solutions, London. An award winning boutique practice focusing on residential work with some commercial. Each project is individually conceived and unique to each client. Recent work includes the complete reconfiguration of a flat in central London to create a home with a detailed 17th century French style, five floors of a commercial space in London to become treatment rooms, offices and meditation spaces plus an apartment in Bucharest.

Rui Ribeiro

Company: Rui Ribeiro Interiors, London. Current projects include a suite at The Albany, Piccadilly, a barn conversion and an apartment in a 19th century building in Lisbon. Rui's design philosophy is to balance the client's interests, the location and the architecture of each home.

Nini Andrade Silva

Company: Atelier Nini Andrade Silva, Funchal, Portugal. With a portfolio of unique award winning interior design projects, Nini's work has been frequently featured in design, architecture, lifestyle, travel and fashion publications.

Commissions vary and include offices, residential, retail, hospitality and exhibition stands worldwide. Nini has also developed unique pieces of furniture for international brands with design collections. Recent work includes the Palais Schwarzenberg Hotel, Austria, Pinheiros Altos, Golf, Spa & Hotel, Portugal, Bog Hotel, Columbia, Hotel do Sal, Cape Verde, Hotel Eden Residence, France and The Robertson Hotel, Malaysia. Other projects include Hotel Teatro, Portugal, a private house in Ponta do Sol, Madeira Island, Sabores da Ilha restaurant, Madeira Island and Hotel Rio Internacional, Brazil.

Molins Interiors

Designers: Toni Molins, Bernat Marcillas, Juan Molins & Carla Marcillas. Company: Molins Interiors, Barcelona, Spain. Molins Interiors comprises a multi disciplinary group of in house professionals with over 30 years experience in residential and commercial interior design throughout Spain. Current projects include a clinic in Barcelona, a duplex penthouse in the centre of Madrid and a beach house in Ibiza. Recent work includes

the complete redesign of a chain of restaurants in Barcelona, the restoration of a country house in the Pyrenees and a private house in San Sebastian. 'Functionality, warmth, timelessness and attention to detail.'

DE TOTS, SEMPRE
ERÀ EL MILLOR
L QUE MÉS PLAE
US DONI.

EL QUE

GUEU

EN EL

MOMENT

OPORTÚ

Carter Tyberghein

Designers: Patrick Tyberghein and Laura Carter. Company: CarterTyberghein, London. Over the last decade CarterTyberghein have worked on a myriad of projects internationally, ranging from private homes, large luxury residential developments to boutique hotels. Recent projects include the refurbishment of a private residence and pool in Cap d'Antibes, and the renovation of an existing 3 storey

home in Ireland, creating a new extension with guest apartments, pool, gym, sauna, steam rooms, cinema & games rooms. Current work includes the demolition and reconstruction of a listed 5 storey private mews residence in central London, three show apartments at Pan Peninsula, Mill Harbour, London, a private contemporary coastal residence in Jersey and the refurbishment and extension of a private house in Hampstead.

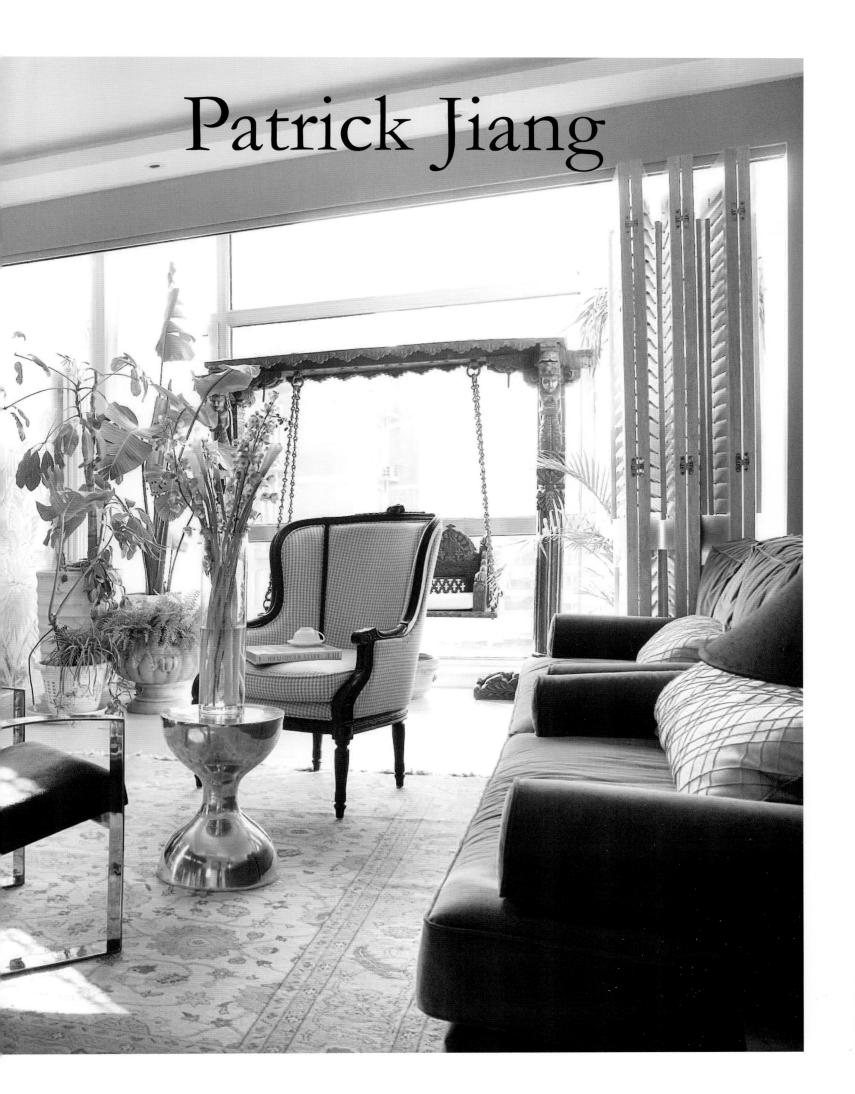

Patrick Jiang

Company: Dara Lifestyle Interior Design, Beijing. Owner and chief designer Patrick Jiang established Dara in 1998 and since then it has become one of the most well known brands in China. Commissions vary and cover the residential, retail, hotel and hospitality sectors. Recent projects include a luxurious private apartment in Beijing and a traditional Quadyard Club combining Chinese, tropical and classic styles.

Hare + Klein

Designer: Meryl Hare. Company: Hare + Klein, Wooloomooloo, Australia. Principal Meryl Hare has 32 years experience in the design industry. She is a Fellow of the Design Institute of Australia, has received a citation for services to the Design Industry and was inducted to the DIA Hall of Fame in 2011. Currently she is National President of the SIDA Foundation. Recent projects include a new spa on Hamilton Island, Great Barrier Reef and an eco lodge in Coledale.

Mirka McNeill

Company: Mirka McNeill Interiors, London. Predominantly residential interiors in the UK. Recent work includes the redesign of a Victorian house in Barnes, the refurbishment of a mews house in Belgravia, an apartment in Ealing and a house in Hertfordshire.

Jeremy Scarlett

Company: RDD Interior Architectural Design Ltd, London. In 1985, after fifteen years working in the fields of exhibition, office, hotel and leisure design, Richard Daniels formed Richard Daniels Design. Now known as RDD Interior Architectural Design Ltd, the company is one of the industry's leading Hotel and Leisure Design practices. RDD are currently undertaking projects for international hotel groups including Rocco Forte Hotels, Intercontinental Hotel Group, Marriott

Hotel, Guoman (Thistle) Hotels and several private clients including AB Hotels, Dartmouth Land Co, Luxury Hotel Partners Ltd, as well as restaurants, bars, and private residences. Recent work includes the refurbishment of 82 guestrooms at the Grade II listed Arch Hotel, London, HUNter 486 (named after the Marylebone direct-dialling code of the 1950's) comprising cocktail bar, Salon de Champagne, Kitchen restaurant and Martini Library, The Augustine Hotel, Prague, including the 13th century Augustinian monastery and a brewery, Hotel Verta, Battersea, London, Five Lakes Hotel, Golf, Country Club & Spa, Maldon, Essex, The Marriott Hotel, Prague and the renovation of Hanbury Manor, Hertfordshire.

Joanna Wood

Company: Joanna Trading, London. Joanna Trading is a dynamic, award winning interior design practice spearheaded by Joanna Wood. The company employs a large team of designers who work with a broad spectrum of clients across the globe. Recent projects include the conversion of four flats in Kensington into a 17,000 sq ft house, a contemporary riverside apartment and a chalet in Verbier. Current work includes one of the largest restoration projects in the South of England, a contemporary Knightsbridge penthouse and the refurbishment of an historic house in Cambridge.

Kathleen Hay

Company: Kathleen Hay Designs, Massachusets, U.S.A.
Residential and commercial and custom graphic design.
Recent work includes a restaurant on Nantucket, a
summer retreat styled as the interior of a ship and a
family estate in the coastal town of Marblehead.
Current projects include a 15,000 sq ft log cabin in
Vermont, a winter residence in Palm Beach and a
waterfront home on the north shore of Nantucket.

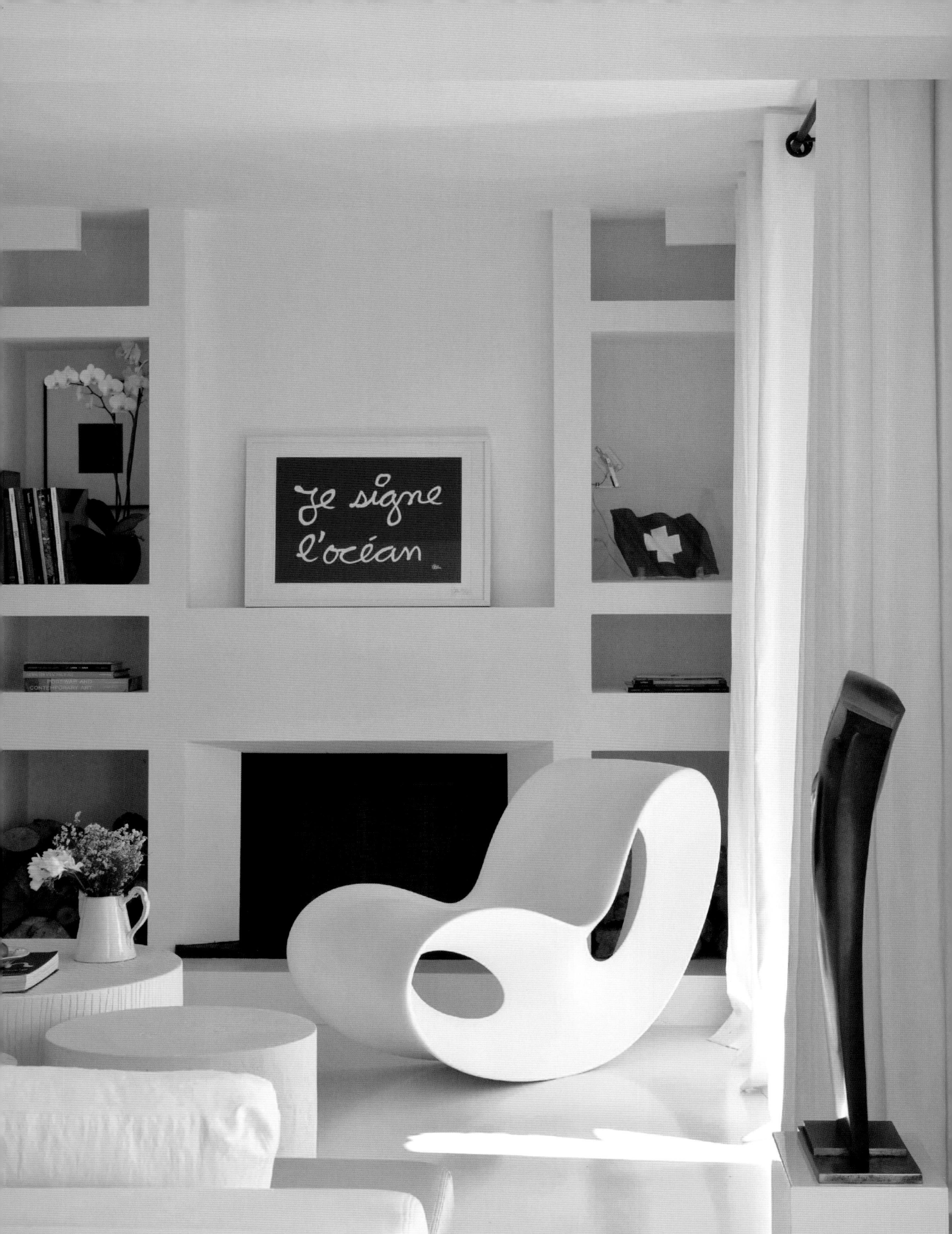
Je signe
l'océan

Federica Palacios

Company: Federica Palacios Design, Geneva, Switzerland. Federica's design philosophy is to create timeless interiors which incorporate her clients' needs and individuality. Work is international, including residential and boutique hotels. Recent projects include a beach front house in Greece, a chalet in Gstaad and a house on the French Riviera. Current work includes a duplex in Geneva, a town house in London and a golf and spa hotel in Tuscany.

Purple Design

Designer: Orla Collins. Company: Purple Design, London. An award winning interior architecture and design practice specialising in tailor made residential houses and apartments in the UK and abroad. Current projects include a contemporary new build luxury house with two subterranean levels and the refurbishment of a large period family house. Recent work includes the complete refurbishment of a house in Wimbledon and apartments in Kensington and Chelsea. 'Attention to detail without compromise.'

Casa do Passadico

Designers: Catarina Rosas, Claudia Soares Pereira & Catarina Soares Pereira. Company: Casa do Passadiço, Porto, Portugal. Recent work includes the restoration of an apartment in an ancient Hotel Particulier in Saint Germain des Pres, Paris, the renovation of several homes in the historical centre of Lisbon, an 18th century manor house in northern Portugal plus several offices for a financial firm and show houses for a prestigious construction company. Currently there are 20 projects underway; they include predominantly private residences in Porto, the Algarve, Lisbon and Estoril as well as the interior design and furnishing of a 40 m private yacht and the design and interior architecture of a luxury brand fashion store in Porto.

Daun Curry

Company: Modern Declaration, New York. A boutique firm offering a full design service for residential and commercial clients. Current work includes a four bedroom family flat that incorporates interior and exterior landscape, overlooking Central Park, a Chelsea duplex loft for international dj, model and socialite Sky Nellor and a modern style Tribeca loft for an avid art collector. Recent projects include the corporate office and showroom for luxury beauty giant Moroccan Oil and a seven bedroom urban estate on Manhattans upper east side, complete with library, private screening room and luxury playroom. 'Forge ahead, appreciate the past.'

Christopher Dezille

Company: Honky, London. An award winning practice specialising in interior architecture & luxury bespoke design for private clients and developers. Recent projects include a duplex penthouse, an apartment in Kensington and a private residence in Cannes. Current work includes a landmark residential development in London, the redevelopment of a substantial family home and the refurbishment of a residential building in Knightsbridge. Honky's design philosophy is about getting the core element of a project right, then everything else should naturally follow.

Geometry Design

Designer: Irina Glik. Company: Geometry Design, Moscow. Primarily restaurant interiors, public spaces and luxury private residences in Russia and overseas. Recent work in Moscow includes GQ Bar, Mr Lee and Tatter Club. Current projects include the Novikov restaurant and bar, London, La Bottega Siciliana di Nino Graziano, Moscow and Black Bean, Moscow.

Curtis Davenport-Woods

Company: Davenport Woods Design, London. Specialising in high end residential projects, private yachts and aircraft. Current work includes a house and apartment in Mayfair and the concept for a 60 metre private yacht. Recent projects include a Kensington apartment and a Mayfair townhouse.

Natalia Belongova

Company: NB-Studio, Moscow. Founded in 2005 by Natalia Belongova, NB-Studio specialises in interior design and photo installations. Recent work includes the offices of Yota, the largest Russian multimedia company, a private villa in Moscow, a family home and the design of a concept store "Project 3/14" located in an old building within the historic heart of Moscow. Current work includes offices for a tobacco company and a young multimedia company plus a private apartment, all in Moscow. NB-Studio's design philosophy is that work is not a job, it's a way of life.

Laura Brucco

Company: Laura Brucco, Buenos Aires, Argentina. Specialising in high end residential and commercial projects including interior architecture and design. Current work includes city apartments, a private residence and farmhouses.

Angelos Angelopoulos

Company: Angelos Angelopoulos Interior Design, Athens, Greece. In 1990 Angelos Angelopoulos designed his first hotel, Andromeda Athens and since then he has designed the interiors of more than 40 predominantly boutique hotels. Work is international including private residences, apartments, restaurants, clubs and showrooms. Current projects include a residential complex and a business park in Cyprus plus a restaurant in Miami. Recent work includes a holiday home on a Greek island, a hotel near the Ionian Sea and a residence in Athens.

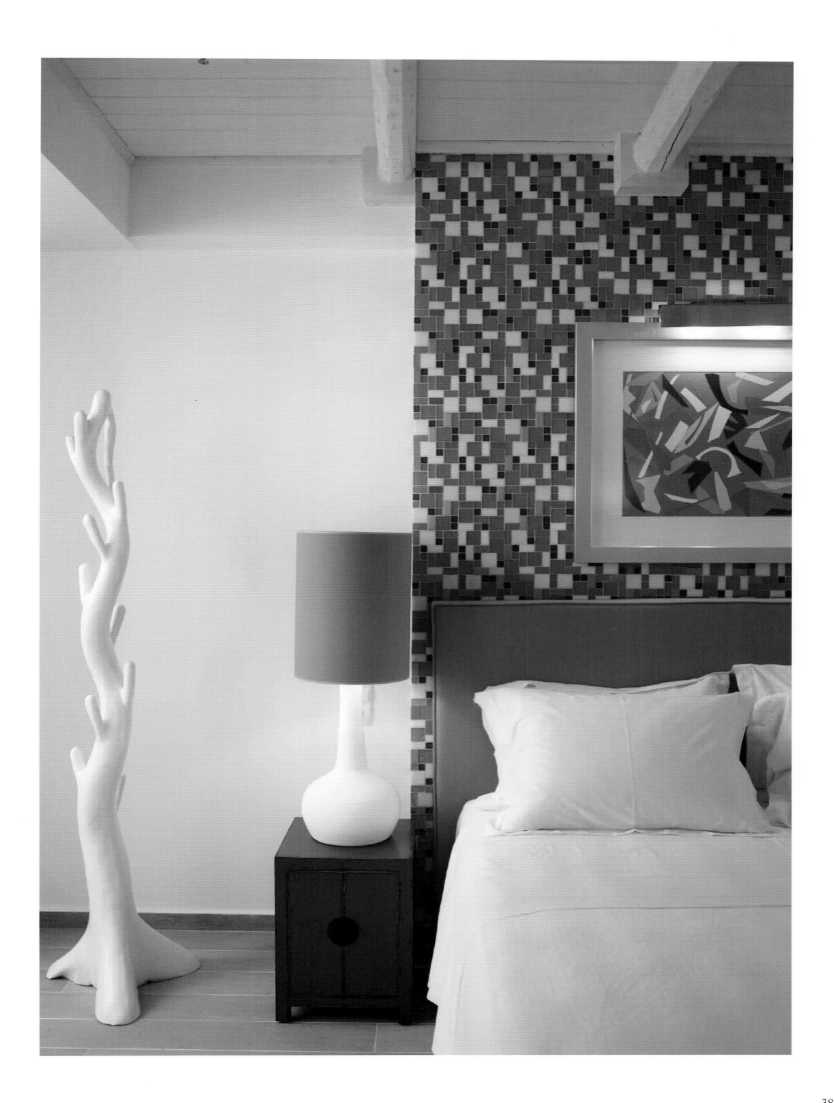

Forward Architecture & Design

Designers: Marco Teixeira & Alexandre Lima. Company: Forward Architecture & Design, Lisbon, Portugal. With a specialised and multi disciplinary team of international professionals, Forward create unique projects that are sensitive to environmental and sustainability concerns.

Recent work includes private houses and a real estate office in Lisbon plus a hotel in Brazil and a technology centre in Lisbon. 'We are today what we did in the past.'

David Muirhead

Company: David Muirhead and Associates, Johannesburg, South Africa. Specialising in residential interior architecture, corporate lodges and exclusive hospitality projects worldwide. A key component in their style is designing to meet their client's needs, whether contemporary or classical. Recent projects include a Karoo farmhouse, a Camps Bay penthouse, a private game lodge and five star hotel commissions. Current work includes executive offices for a European investment company plus various private residences ranging from a Victorian mansion to a beach house. David's design philosophy is to keep design simple with integrity.

Jorge Cañete

Company: Interior Design Philosophy, Vaud, Switzerland. After carrying out a number of projects in the offices of architects in Rome and Geneva, Jorge Cañete founded his own design studio. Jorge's characteristic style mixes modernity with poetry. Recent work includes a villa near Lake Geneva, a contemporary art exhibition for Swiss artist Peter Wüthrich and an exhibition stand for a prestigious watchmaker at Baselworld. Current projects include a castle in Northern Europe, a traditional mansion in Geneva and a private apartment in Spain. Jorge's design philosophy is to carefully analyse his three sources of inspiration: the environment surrounding a project, the feeling inherent in the location and the client's own personality.

Antoni Associates

Designers: Mark Rielly, Vanessa Weissenstein, Ashleigh Gilmour and Jon Case. Company: Antoni Associates, Cape Town, South Africa. Projects are predominantly in South Africa but also in Paris, Moscow, London and Geneva. Work includes domestic, hospitality, retail, corporate and leisure sectors. Led by Mark Rielly and Vanessa Weissenstein, Antoni Associates prides itself on its dedication to cutting edge and bespoke contemporary design coupled with sound technical knowledge. Recent projects include Radisson Blu Hotel, Dakar and private residences in Geneva and Dar es Salaam. Current work includes a villa on Palm Jumeirah, Dubai, a private residence in London and another on Eden Island, Seychelles.

Mary Gannon

Designers: Mary Gannon and Senior Design Associate Cynthia Garcia. Company: Mary Gannon Design, London. Chelsea based company specialising in bespoke residential work with some commercial interior design commissions. Clients include private individuals and property and hotel developers both in the UK and abroad. Recent projects include the refurbishment of an apartment for the Master of the Royal Armouries at the Tower of London, a room in tribute to Jimi Hendrix at the Cumberland Hotel, London and a cutting edge home filled with the latest technology, working in conjunction with Toh Shimazaki Architects. Current work includes homes in Knightsbridge and Hampton Hill plus twelve executive buy to let apartments.

Brian Leib

Company: Brian Leib Interiors, Cape Town, South Africa. Specialising in 'from the ground up' projects for the last 22 years. Recent work includes a 2600 sq m private residence in Cape Town, a chateau styled project in Durban and a 10 suite boutique hotel in Johannesburg. Current projects include a sky rise penthouse in Johannesburg, a private home for an African statesman and a mansion in Ibiza.

Rachel Laxer

Company: Rachel Laxer Interiors, London and New York. Working on large scale projects worldwide, in collaboration with F3 Architects and Design, London. Recent work includes the complete renovation of a penthouse flat in central London, the construction of a classic brick and limestone Georgian Estate property in Westchester, NY, the build and installation of a modern home in Silicon Valley and the interior design of a classic period home with a blend of English Regency and Art Deco in Westchester, NY. Current projects include the interior design and renovation of a family home in Hertfordshire, England, the construction of a ski chalet in the European Alps, the design of a family home in an upper west side penthouse in NYC, the interior of a family home in a listed North London Georgian house and the updating of a holiday home in the South of France.

Terence Disdale

Company: Terence Disdale Design Limited, Richmond, UK. One of the world's leading, award winning yacht designers specialising in the exterior and interior design of superyachts and luxury motor and sailing yachts. Since 1980 over sixty five yachts, between 30-140 m have been completed to Disdale Design drawings and specifications and the company has been recognised for its significant contribution to the design of the

largest yachts to be delivered to date. The 21st century continues to keep the studio busy with another seven motor yachts in production ranging between 62-162 metres. Recent projects include a 53.5 m motor yacht Hurricane Run, an 85.5 m motor yacht Sunrays, a new build which recently received the International Superyacht Society Award for Best Yacht in Category and a 163.5 m motor yacht Eclipse, which received World Superyacht Awards for Best Boat in Category and Best Boat of the Year. Eclipse is currently the largest private yacht in the world.

Enrica Fiorentini Delpani

Company: Studio Giardino, Brescia, Italy. The name Studio Giardino derives from the association of Carlo Fiorentini who is responsible for lighting installation and landscape gardening and Enrica Fiorentini Delpani who deals with interior and exterior design and architecture. Recent projects include the restoration of an old house, the restructuring of a hotel and the renovation and complete furnishing of a house near Cortina d'Ampezzo, in Sappada.

Current work includes an apartment in the historic centre of Milan, a villa in the hills and a hotel on Lake Garda. Enrica's design mantra is to refurbish with respect, finding timeless solutions.

Linda Steen

Company: AS Scenario, Oslo, Norway. Established in 1985 by Linda Steen, today the office has a broadly experienced international staff of 26 including interior designers, furniture designers and administrators. Recent projects include the creation of office and recreational space to represent Flytoget, the airport express train in Oslo, the design of offices for the bank Terra-Gruppen and a 650 sq ft new office space for the Scenario team. Current projects include Rica Hotel Narvik, Aker Solutions Interior project for an engineering and construction group and Deichmanske Bibliotek interior for the National library.

Suite Home
Interiors

Designers: Polina Belyakova, Ekaterina Kotova & Ekaterina Ponyatovskaya. Company: Suite Home Interiors, Moscow, Russia. With experience in publishing, finance, PR, photography and history of art, Polina and Ekaterina are graduates of the Russian interior design school 'Details' and postgraduates of the KLC School of Design in London. They have worked together for over 5 years and designed the interiors of apartments, houses, restaurants, cafes and offices. Their work has been published in various magazines: AD, Elle Decor, Mezonin, Seasons and Interior+Design. Recent projects are in Moscow and include a timber framed country house, an apartment and a restaurant. Current work includes two modern apartments and a country estate near Tula, outside Moscow.

One Plus Partnership

Designers: Ajax Law & Virginia Lung. Company: One Plus Partnership, North Point, Hong Kong. Established in 2004 by directors Ajax Law and Virginia Lung, One Plus Partnership Limited is a young interior design firm with a growing reputation for cutting edge interiors in show flats, club houses, retail stores, penthouses, public spaces and offices, both locally and internationally. They have received numerous industry awards and accolades. Recent work includes Yoho Midtown Residential Clubhouse, Shanghai IFC Mall Palace cinema and Chongqing Forte, Cullinan show flat. Current projects include a Nova City sales office and clubhouse, a cinema and a Chongqing sales office and show flat. 'Life enhancing design for every project.'

Hill House

Designers: Jenny Weiss & Helen Bygraves. Company: Hill House Interiors, Weybridge, Surrey. Majoring in luxury residential projects, hotels and restaurants in the UK and worldwide. Recent work includes a private estate in La Zagaleta, Spain, a penthouse in Mayfair and a restaurant in Bratislava, Slovakia. Current projects include a boutique hotel in Cornwall, a private villa in Antibes and a London residence for a Royal family in Highgate.

Chen Bin

Company: China Root (Hubei) Hosun Design Consultancy, China. Specialising in the interior design and planning of hotels, restaurants and high end clubs, real estate projects and offices. Recent work includes a Hankou mansion, the renovation of a period house and a boutique.

Fiona Barratt

Company: Fiona Barratt Interiors, London. A successful studio working on high end projects in the UK and Europe for both private and commercial clients. Recent work includes the substantial conversion of a 400 year old watermill to include two swimming pools and two cinemas, the complete renovation of a Georgian hall into a 24,000 sq ft residence with swimming pool and 2,500 sq ft modern kitchen with 9 m ceilings and a floating mezzanine, plus a new build beach villa in Mallorca.

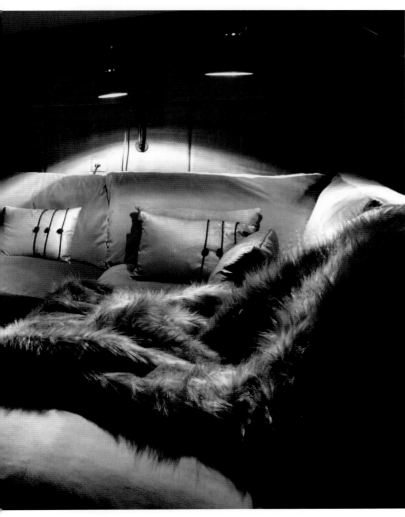

Alla Shumeyko

Company: Alla Décor-studio, Moscow, Russia. Alla Décor specialise in the design and decoration of private and public interiors including furniture and accessories predominantly in Russia. They have recently completed a private apartment, a restaurant and a country house. Current work includes a private residence and apartments in Moscow. 'Individuality, comfort, harmony.'

Patrick Leung

Company: PAL Design Consultants, Causeway Bay, Hong Kong. An award winning company established in 1994. PAL is one of the largest interior design firms in Greater China, with a team of over 80 staff distributed over four offices; Hong Kong, Beijing, Shanghai and Shenzhen. Specialising in a full design service for all categories of large scale projects. Recent work in China includes Narada Villa and Resort, Hainan and Mission Hills Golf Resorts in Haikou and Dongguan. Current projects include Hilton Nanjing Hotel, Sheraton Hotel, Xiao Shing and Marriott executive apartments, Shenzhen. 'Original, spiritual, eternal.'

Christian's & Hennie

Designer: Helene Hennie. Company: Christian's & Hennie, Oslo, Norway. Working on a broad range of high end residential projects throughout Norway as well as internationally. Examples include private homes, summer cabins and winter lodges, to more industrial projects such as restaurants, hotels and offices. Their style varies from modern to classical. Recent work includes a mountain lodge, a city apartment and a coastal holiday home, plus an apartment in London, a corporate office space and a restaurant in Dubai.

Glamorous

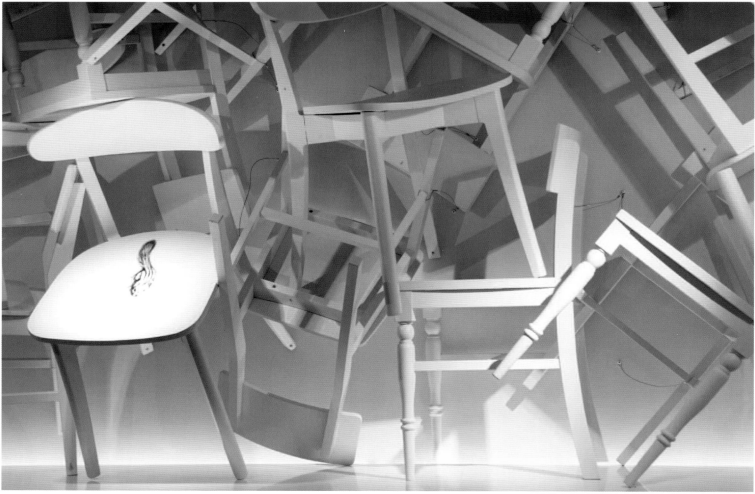

Designer: Yasumichi Morita. Company: Glamorous, Tokyo, Japan. Established in 2000 by Yasumichi Morita. Since his first project in Hong Kong in 2001 he has expanded to many cities including New York, London and Shanghai offering graphic and product design as well as interior design for restaurants, retail stores, hotels, resort complexes and various residences. Recent work includes the Waterside Macau 'Apex Collection', Brillia Ariake Skytower and the Glamorous Tokyo office. Current projects include Gogaibo Hotel in Shanghai, commercial space project in Shanghai Shintian-di and a restaurant project in Hong Kong.

254 Manuel Francisco Jorge
Manuel Francisco Jorge Interior Design Studios
Rua S. Domingos Domingos A Lapa, 1/7
R/CDTO
1200 - 834 Lisbon
studio@manuelfranciscojorge.com
Tel +351 213 424 294
Fax +351 917 277 318
www.manuelfrancisco.com

258 Carl Emil Erikson
Carl Emil Erikson Design
PO BOX 633
SE-101 32 Stockholm, Sweden
info@carlemilerikson.com
France +33 (0)642 586 868
Sweden +46 (0) 708 960 200
Fax +46 (0) 708 960 264
UK +44 (0) 754 027 7700
www.carlemilerikson.com

262 Geraldine Milsom
Milsom Hotels & Restaurants
Gun Hill
Dedham, Colchester
Essex CO7 6HP
geraldine@milsomhotels.com
Tel +44 1206 323 150
Fax +44 1206 322 309
www.milsomhotels.com

266 Cao Cheng
Shenzhen Hope-Box Surrounding
Design Corporation
3/F West Tower Huamei Building
Zhenxing Road, Futian District
Shenzhen P.R.China
szcaocheng@vip.163.com
Tel +86 755 83248678
Fax +86 755 83216894
www.szhope-box.com

270 Susan Bednar Long
S.B. Long Interiors Inc
9 Benedict Place
Greenwich
CT 06830, USA
info@sblonginteriors.com
Tel +1 203 769 1030
Fax +1 203 769 1028
www.sblonginteriors.com

276 Andrew Dunn & Alex Michelin
Finchatton
25 Ives Street
London SW3 2ND
info@finchatton.com
Tel +44 207 591 2700
Fax +44 207 581 2472
www.finchatton.com

280 Michelle Pabarcius
Design Solutions
14 Langford Place
London NW8 OLL
michelle@mp-designsolutions.co.uk
Tel +44 207 604 4701
Fax +44 207 604 4701
www.mp-designsolutions.co.uk

286 Rui Ribeiro
Rui Ribeiro Interiors
2-4 Great Eastern Street
London
EC2A 3NT
info@ruiribeirointeriors.com
Mobile +44 771 705 5442
Fax +44 207 584 2646
www.ruiribeirointeriors.com

290 Nini Andrade Silva
Atelier Nini Andrade Silva
Rua Princesa D Amelia No 1
9000 - 019 Funchal
Madeira, Portugal
esboco@esboco.com
Tel +351 291 204 370
Fax +351 291 204 379
www.niniandradesilva.com

294 Toni Molins, Bernat Marcillas,
Juan Molins & Carla Marcillas
Molins Interiors
C/ Maria Auxiliadora, 17
Barcelona 08017
molinsinteriors@molinsinteriors.com
Tel +34 93 205 25 56
Fax +34 93 203 19 07
www.molinsinteriors.com

298 Patrick Tyberghein
Carter Tyberghein
Hyde Park House
Manfred Road, 5
London SW15 2RS
info@cartertyberghein.com
Tel +44 208 871 4800
Fax +44 208 871 4900
www.cartertyberghein.com

302 Patrick Jiang
Dara Lifestyle Interior Design & Home Living
798 Art District No 2
Jiuxianqiao Chaoyang District
Beijing
dara.jiangpeng@gmail.com
Tel +86 10 59 78 9701
www.dara.com.cn

306 Meryl Hare
Hare + Klein
Level 1, 91 Bourke Street
Wooloomooloo
NSW 2011 Australia
info@hareklein.com.au
Tel +61 2 9368 1234
Fax +61 2 9368 1020
www.hareklein.com.au

312 Mirka McNeill Farmer
Mirka Mcneill Interiors
22 Elm Grove Road
Barnes
London SW13 OBT
mirkamcneill@gmail.com
Tel +44 208 878 2641
Fax +44 208 878 2641
www.mirkamcneill.com

318 Jeremy Scarlett
RDD Interior Architectural Design Ltd
Battersea Studios
Studio G8
80 Silverthorne Road
Battersea
London SW8 3HE
jscarlett@rdd.uk.com
Tel +44 208 767 8428
www.rdd.uk.com

324 Joanna Wood
Joanna Trading Interior Design
7 Bunhouse Place
London SW1W 8HU
Tel +44 207 730 0695
Fax +44 207 730 4135
joannaw@joannawood.com
www.joannatrading.com

328 Kathleen Hay
Kathleen Hay Designs
PO Box 801, Nantucket
MA 02554
USA
info@kathleenhaydesigns.com
Tel +1 508 228 1219
Fax +1 508 228 6366
www.kathleenhaydesigns.com

332 Federica Palacios
Federica Palacios Design
Cour St Pierre 3
1204 Geneva
Switzerland
federica@federicapalaciosdesign.com
Tel +41 22 310 2276
Fax +41 22 310 22 86
www.federicapalaciosdesign.com

338 Orla Collins
Purple Design Ltd
The Old Gasworks
Uint H2 Capital House
2 Michael Road
London SW6 2YH
Info@purple-design.co.uk
Tel +44 207 736 4464
Fax +44 871 989 8817
www.purple-design.co.uk

342 Catarina Rosas, Claudia Soares Pereira &
Catarina Soares Pereira
Casa do Passadiço Interiors
Largo de S. Joao do Souto
4700 326 Braga, Portugal
mail@casadopassadico.com
Tel +351 253 619988
Fax +351 253 213 110
www.casadopassadico.com

346 Daun Curry
Modern Declaration
37 Wall Street
Suite 11B, New York
NY 10005 USA
info@moderndeclaration.com
Tel +1 212 480 2593
Fax +1 212 937 3117
www.moderndeclaration.com

350 Christopher Dezille
Honky
Unit 1 Pavement Studios
40-48 Bromells Road
London SW4 OBG
chris@honky.co.uk
Tel +44 207 622 7144
Fax +44 207 622 7155
www.honky.co.uk

356 Irina Glik
Geometry Design
Kutuzovsky Prospect, 45
Bld 1, Moscow
Russia 121170
geometry-moscow@mail.ru
Tel +7 495 771 70 41
Fax +7 495 771 70 41

360 Curtis Davenport-Woods
Davenport Woods Designs
Office 404
Albany House
342 Regent Street
London W1B 3HH
hello@davenport.woods.com
Tel +44 7545 178 039
www.davenport.woods.com

366 Natalia Belongova
NB-studio
Serafimovicha St. 2
Moscow, Russia
nb@nb-studio.ru
Tel +791 653 07883
Fax +74 9566 83 707
www.nb-studio.ru

370 Laura Brucco
Laura Brucco
Metropolitan Museum
Castex 3217, 1st Floor
C1425 CDC Buenos Aires, Argentina
estudio@laurabrucco.com
Tel +5411 4808 9565
www.laurabrucco.com

376 Angelos Angelopoulos
Angelos Angelopoulos Interior Designer
5 Proairessiou Str, 116 36 Mets
Athens, Greece
design@angelosangelopoulos.com
Tel/Fax +30 210 756 7191
www.angelosangelopoulos.com

382 Marco Teixeira & Alexandre Lima
Forward Architecture & Interior Design
Rua Joao Penha No 14 - A
1250-131 Lisbon, Portugal
marco@forward-aid.com
Tel +351 213 828 400
www.forward-aid.com

386 David Muirhead
David Muirhead & Associates
PO BOX 413544
Craighall Park, Johannesburg
South Africa
david@davidmuirheadid.co.za
Tel +27 11 784 5555
Fax +27 11 784 5051
www.davidmuirhead.com

392 Jorge Cañete
Interior Design Philosophy
Chateau d'Hauteville - Aile Est
1806 Saint - Legier
Switzerland
info@jorgecanete.com
Tel +41 78 710 25 34
Fax +41 21 944 37 57
www.jorgecanete.com

398 Mark Rielly
Antoni Associates
109 Hatfield Street Gardens
Cape Town
mark@aainteriors.co.za
Tel +27 21 468 4400
Fax +27 21 461 5408
www.aainteriors.co.za

406 Mary Gannon
Mary Gannon Design
Top Floor, Chelsea Reach
79-89 Lots Road
London SW10 ORN
mary@marygannondesign.co.uk
Tel/Fax +44 207 823 3355
Mobile +44 7952 066607
www.marygannondesign.co.uk

410 Brian Leib
Brian Leib Interiors
No 107 Heather Avenue
Athol, Johannesburg
2196 South Africa
info@blinteriors.co.za
Tel +27 11 444 5505
Fax +27 11 444 6373
www.brianleibinteriors.com

416 Rachel Laxer
Rachel Laxer Interiors
8 Harmood Grove, Camden
London NW1 8DH
rlaxerinteriors@aol.com
Tel +44 207 267 8332/+44 7545 927 771
www.rlaxerinteriors.com

420 Terence Disdale
Terence Disdale Design Limited
6 The Green
Richmond
Surrey TW9 1PL
terencedisdale@terencedisdale.co.uk
Tel +44 208 940 1452
Fax +44 208 940 5964
www.terencedisdaledesign.co.uk

426 Enrica Fiorentini Delpani
Studio Giardino
Via Caselle 6
25100, Brescia, Italy
studiogiardino55@libero.it
Tel +39 030 353 2548
Fax +39 030 353 2548
www.studiogiardino.com

432 Linda Steen
As Scenario Interiørarkitekter MNIL
Piestredet 75c
0354 0510 - Norway
ls@scenario.no
Tel +47 928 93 000
www.scenario.no

438 Polina Belyakova, Ekaterina Kotova &
Ekaterina Ponyatovskaya
Suite Home Interiors
103062 Pokrovka Str 47/24
Moscow, Russia
suitehome@mail.ru
Tel +7 985 970 5617
www.suitehome.ru

444 Ajax Law & Virginia Lung
One Plus Partnership Ltd
9/F New Wing
101 King's Road, North Point
Hong Kong
vl@onepluspartnership.com
Tel +852 259 19308
Fax +852 259 19362
www.onepluspartnership.com

452 Jenny Weiss & Helen Bygraves
Hill House Interiors
32-34 Baker Street
Weybridge
Surrey KT13 8AT
jenny@hillhouseinteriors.com
Tel +44 1932 858 900
Fax +44 1932 858 997
www.hillhouseinteriors.com

458 Chen Bin
China Root (Hubei) Hosun Design Consultants
368 # Zhong Shan Road
Wuhan City
Hubei Province, China
cl-vip@163.com
Tel +86 27 888 72039
Fax +86 27 888 72039

462 Fiona Barratt
Fiona Barratt Interiors
The Library, The 1927 Building
2 Michael Road
London SW6 2AD
info@fionabarrattinteriors.com
Tel +44 207 731 3600
www.fionabarrattinteriors.com

468 Alla Shumeyko
Alla Décor Studio
Kosmodemiansky Str 7/3 - 261
125130 Moscow, Russia
alla.decor@mail.ru
Tel +7 903 770 8717
www.alladecor.ru

474 Patrick Leung
PAL Design Consultants
Penthouse, Chinachem Leighton Plaza
29 Leighton Road
Causeway Bay, Hong Kong
hongkong@paldesign.cn
Tel +852 2877 1233
Fax +852 2824 9275
www.paldesign.cn

482 Helene Hennie
Christian's & Hennie AS
Skovveien 6
N - 0257 Oslo, Norway
info@christiansoghennie.no
Tel +47 22 12 13 50
Fax +47 22 12 13 51
www.christiansoghennie.no

486 Yasumichi Morita
Glamorous Co Ltd
2F 2-7-25 Motoazabu, Minato-Ku
Tokyo 106-0046, Japan
info@glamorous.co.jp
Tel +81 03 5475 1037
Fax +81 03 5475 1038
www.glamorous.co.jp

© 2011 Andrew Martin International

Second Printing

Editor Martin Waller
Project Executive Annika Bowman
Design by Graphicom Design

Production by Nele Jansen, teNeues Verlag
Editorial coordination by Inga Wortmann, teNeues Verlag
Colour separation by SPM Print

First published in 2011 by teNeues Verlag GmbH + Co. KG, Kempen

teNeues Verlag GmbH + Co. KG
Am Selder 37, 47906 Kempen, Germany
Phone: +49-(0)2152-916-0
Fax: +49-(0)2152-916-111
e-mail: books@teneues.de

Press department: Andrea Rehn
Phone: +49-(0)2152-916-202
e-mail: arehn@teneues.de

teNeues Digital Media GmbH
Kohlfurter Straße 41–43, 10999 Berlin, Germany
Phone: +49-(0)30-7007765-0

www.teneues.com

teNeues Publishing Company
7 West 18th Street, New York, NY 10011, USA
Phone: +1-212-627-9090
Fax: +1-212-627-9511

teNeues Publishing UK Ltd.
21 Marlowe Court, Lymer Avenue, London SE19 1LP, UK
Phone: +44-(0)20-8670-7522
Fax: +44-(0)20-8670-7523

teNeues France S.A.R.L
39, rue des Billets, 18250 Henrichemont, France
Phone: +33-(0)2-4826-9348
Fax: +33-(0)1-7072-3482

Andrew Martin trade edition: ISBN 978-0-9558938-3-4
teNeues trade edition: ISBN 978-3-8327-9597-9
Library of Congress Control Number: 2011933953
Printed in the Czech Republic

Bibliographic information published by the Deutsche Nationalbibliothek.
The Deutsche Nationalbibliothek lists this publication in the Deutsche Nationalbibliografie; detailed bibliographic data are available in the Internet at http://dnb.d-nb.de.

Acknowledgments

The author and publisher wish to thank all the owners and designers of the projects featured in this book.

They also thank the following photographers:

Wentao She, Jonathan Root, Marcus Peel, Mel Yates, Adriaan Campbell Louw, Aleksandra Laska, Hanna Dlugosz, Pawel Zak, The Dorchester Hotel, Peter Vanderwarker, Kwes Arthur, Kevin Lein, Matthew Millman, Prue Ruscoe, Michele Biancucci, Satoru Umetsu of Nacasa & Partners Inc., Philp Vile, Peter Bennett, Bruce Thomas, Gregory Maillot, Klaus Lorke, Niall Clutton, Piranha Photography London, Ray Main, Marco Blessano, Nacasa & Partners Inc, Earl Carter, Anson Smart, Steve Back, Steve Russell Studios, Antonio Moutinho, Mikhail Stepanov, Nina Dreyer Hensley & Jim Hensley www.dreyerhensley.com, Anne Manglerud www.annemanglerud.no, Daniel Hase, Kiril Ovchinnikov, Frank Herfort, Elisa Venturelli, Giorgio Baroni, Pavlos Tsokounoglou, Jonathan Shapiro, Grey Crawford, Angie Silvy, Skye Moorhead, Dmitriy Livshitz, Evgeniy Luchin, Antonio Teixeira, Jose Luis Dias, Giorgio Baroni, Dominic Blackmore, Steve Nge of Trizone, Edward Hendricks of CI&A Photography, Silvio Rech, Dook, Keisuke Miyamoto, Martin Clairmont, Mark Williams, Jason Busch www.jasonbusch.com, Marco Antonio, Manuel Gomes da Costa, Leoppard Liu, Michael Paul, Gavin Kingcombe, Caroline True, David Marlow, Emily Minton Redfield, Marc Gerritsen, An Li, Chou Yu-Hsien, Raphael Faux gstaadphotography.com, Sergey Ananiev, Amy Murrell www.amymurrel.co.uk, Rocco Forte Hotels www.roccofortehotels.com, von Essen Hotels www.vonessenhotels.co.uk, Peter Tjahjadi, Paul Barbera, Shou-Shan Lai, Chun-Chieh Liu, Jose Miguel Figueiredo, Johan Carlson, Robert Leveritt, Wilson (Thailand), Bryan Rowland, Susan Bednar Long, Richard Waite, Luke White, Andreas von Einsiedel, Nickolas Bayntun, Jordi Miralles & Lluis Sans, Patrick Tyberghein, Sanshou, Yun Wei, Anson Smart, Jeremy Scarlett, Sanjit Bahra, Heiner Orth, Jeffrey Allen, Gilles Trillard, Adam Butler, Carlos Ramos, Francisco Almeida Dias, William Wesbster, Emily Gilbert, Simon Winson, Warren Smith, Elena Koldunova, Vladimir Klyosov, Andrey Nikolskiy, Daniela Mac Adden, Vangelis Paterakis, Kostas Mitropoulos, Alexandre Lima, Vanessa Lewis, David Nemeth, Mark Lanning, Gunther Grater, Top Billing, Eric Rakotomalala, Christine Besson, Xavier Voirol, Adam Letch, Elsa Young, Jonathan Paul Case, Niall Clutton, Zahurul Islam, Hans Fonk, Elsa Young, Jo Pawels, Shivi Islam, Gwen Shabka www.gwenshabka.net, www.marchantandgonta.com, Robert Marchant, Christopher Gonta, Richard Seaton, Umberto Favretto, Gatis Rozenfelds, William Webster, Ajax Law Ling Kit, Virginia Lung, Thierry Cardineau, Wu Hui, Mikhail Stepanov, Bobby Sum, Bao Sze Wang, Charlie Xia, Morten Andenaes, Nacasa & Partners, Seiryo Studio, Courtesy of Zetton, I. Susa.